# BAKERS
## MAKE MANY THINGS

**Photo Credits:**
© Chad Slattery/Tony Stone Images: cover
© Don Smetzer/Tony Stone Images: 3, 22
© Gregg Andersen/Gallery 19: 10, 20, 28, 30
© Jack McConnell: 4, 16, 24
© Mark Williams/Tony Stone Images: 18
© Michael Rosenfeld/Tony Stone Images: 8, 12, 14
© Rene Sheret/Tony Stone Images: 26
© Steven Rothfeld/Tony Stone Images: 6

**Library of Congress Cataloging-in-Publication Data**

Greene, Carol.

Bakers make many things/by Carol Greene.
p.    cm.
Summary: Describes, in simple text
and photographs, the jobs of the various
people who work in a bakery.
ISBN 1-56766-559-4 (lib. bdg. : alk. paper)
1. Bakers and bakeries—Juvenile literature.
2. Baking—Juvenile literature.
[1. Bakers and bakeries.  2. Occupations.]  I. Title.

| TX763.G6525 | 1998 | 98-3108 |
|---|---|---|
| 664'.752—dc21 | | CIP |
| | | AC |

# BAKERS
# MAKE MANY THINGS

**By Carol Greene**

**The Child's World®, Inc.**

4

# MMMM!

It is early in the morning. Most people are asleep. But this baker is already hard at work. She has made lots of bread to sell.

Many bakers go to work very early in the morning. That is because baking things takes a long time.

This baker makes rolls and muffins. They must be ready for early breakfasts. He also makes big loaves of bread. They come in many different flavors.

CLATTER!  CLINK!  CLANK!

These bakers work for a big baking company. Big baking companies use many **machines**. They also use lots of pots and pans.

# CLINK! CLANK!

Sometimes the machines break.
Then workers must fix them.

STIR! PAT! CHOP!

These bakers are called production workers. They each have a special job to do. Some make **batter** for cakes. Others cut up fruit to place on top.

**PLOP! PLOP! PLOP!**

Big baking companies make many loaves of bread each day. They make cakes and other baked goods, too.

VROOM!

Truck drivers take the finished goods to grocery stores and supermarkets. There people can buy them to take home.

Some bakers work for smaller companies. They do not use as many machines.

FZZZ!

This baker puts fancy icing on some cakes. She is a **decorator**. Decorating is a tricky job. It takes lots of practice and hard work.

These bakers once worked for a big company. They worked for a smaller company, too. Now they have their own bakery shop.

Bakers in small shops are very busy. Some make lots of things such as breads, rolls, and muffins. Others make only cakes and pies.

This baker works in a big bakery. She has made lots of **pastries** to sell. She places them on a big pan. Now they are ready for people to buy.

# MMMM!

What is that wonderful smell? This baker is baking rolls. She places them on a tall cart. Then the cart is put into a big oven. The rolls are baked until they are nice and brown.

When the rolls are done, the baker takes the cart out of the oven. She lets the rolls cool for a long time.

Then the baker takes the rolls off the cart.
She stacks them carefully. Now they are
ready for everyone to enjoy!

# QUESTIONS AND ANSWERS

## What do bakers do?

Bakers make bread, cakes, cookies, and other bread goods. Some run machines that do part of the work. Others do the whole job themselves.

## How do people learn to be bakers?

Most bakers finish at least high school. They start out as bakery helpers. Baking companies hold classes for them and help them learn on the job. People can also learn to be bakers at some colleges or special schools such as the American Baking Institute.

## What kind of people are bakers?

Bakers must work well with other people. They must be healthy and clean. They must not mind working long days—or getting up early. Most of all, they must like to work with food.

## How much money do bakers make?

Many bakers earn about $20,000 a year. Starting bakers earn less. A baker in a fine restaurant or shop could earn more.

# GLOSSARY

**batter (BA-ter)**
Batter is a thick mixture made with eggs, flour, and milk. When it is baked, it turns into cake or cookies.

**decorator (DEH-ko-ray-ter)**
A decorator uses icing and other things to make bakery products look good.

**machines (muh-SHEENZ)**
Machines are tools that help people do things. Bakers use many different machines.

**pastries (PAY-streez)**
Pastries are sweet treats that bakeries make. Pastries are often made from very thick batter.

# INDEX

CAROL GREENE has published over 200 books for children. She also likes to read books, make teddy bears, work in her garden, and sing. Ms. Greene lives in Webster Groves, Missouri.